Inclusion

HBR EMOTIONAL INTELLIGENCE SERIES

HBR Emotional Intelligence Series

How to be human at work

The HBR Emotional Intelligence Series features smart, essential reading on the human side of professional life from the pages of *Harvard Business Review*.

Authentic Leadership	*Influence and Persuasion*
Confidence	*Leadership Presence*
Dealing with Difficult People	*Mindful Listening*
Empathy	*Mindfulness*
Energy and Motivation	*Power and Impact*
Focus	*Purpose, Meaning, and Passion*
Good Habits	*Resilience*
Happiness	*Self-Awareness*
Inclusion	*Virtual EI*

Other books on emotional intelligence from *Harvard Business Review*:

HBR Everyday Emotional Intelligence

HBR Guide to Emotional Intelligence

HBR's 10 Must Reads on Emotional Intelligence

Inclusion

HBR EMOTIONAL INTELLIGENCE SERIES

Harvard Business Review Press

Boston, Massachusetts

Copyright 2023 Harvard Business School Publishing Corporation
All rights reserved
Printed in the United Kingdom by TJ Books Ltd, Padstow, Cornwall

10 9 8 7 6 5 4 3 2

The web addresses referenced in this book were live and correct at the time of the book's publication but may be subject to change.

Cataloging-in-Publication data is forthcoming.

ISBN: 978-1-64782-482-2
eISBN: 978-1-64782-483-9

The paper used in this publication meets the requirements of the American National Standard for Permanence of Paper for Publications and Documents in Libraries and Archives Z39.48-1992.

Contents

1. **Why Inclusive Leaders Are Good for Organizations**   **1**

   Six behaviors to model when practicing inclusive leadership.

   By Juliet Bourke and Andrea Titus

2. **The Value of Belonging at Work**   **15**

   It's beneficial for people—and for the bottom line.

   By Evan W. Carr, Andrew Reece, Gabriella Rosen Kellerman, and Alexi Robichaux

3. **Make Psychological Safety a Strategic Priority**   **29**

   How leaders can enhance integrity, innovation, and inclusion.

   By Maren Gube and Debra Sabatini Hennelly

Contents

4. **The Importance of Being an Inclusive Colleague** 49

   Small gestures can make a big difference.

   By Juliet Bourke

5. **Recognizing and Responding to Microaggressions** 65

   What to do if you witness one—or commit one yourself.

   By Ella F. Washington

6. **Tap into Empathy** 89

   Treat others how they want to be treated.

   By Irina Cozma

7. **Inclusion Starts with Belonging** 99

   Unlearn your own biases, especially the ones you have against yourself.

   By DDS Dobson-Smith

Contents

8. Stop Using These Words and Phrases   115

The language we use can make others feel hurt, disrespected, and isolated.

By Rakshitha Arni Ravishankar

9. The Power of Sharing Our Stories   131

It's a rare chance to take on a new perspective.

By Selena Rezvani and Stacey A. Gordon

Index   147

Inclusion

HBR EMOTIONAL INTELLIGENCE SERIES

1

Why Inclusive Leaders Are Good for Organizations

By Juliet Bourke and Andrea Titus

Companies increasingly rely on diverse, multi-disciplinary teams that combine the collective capabilities of women and men, people of different cultural heritage, and younger and older workers. But simply throwing a mix of people together doesn't guarantee high performance; it requires *inclusive leadership*—leadership that ensures that all team members feel they are treated respectfully and fairly, are valued and sense that they belong, and are confident and inspired.

Inclusiveness isn't just nice to have on teams. Our research shows that it directly enhances performance.

Teams with inclusive leaders are 17% more likely to report that they are high performing, 20% more likely to say they make high-quality decisions, and 29% more likely to report behaving collaboratively. What's more, we found that a 10% improvement in perceptions of inclusion increases work attendance by almost one day a year per employee, reducing the cost of absenteeism.

What specific actions can leaders take to be more inclusive? To answer this question, we surveyed more than 4,100 employees about inclusion, interviewed those identified by followers as highly inclusive, and reviewed the academic literature on leadership. From this research, we identified 17 discrete sets of behaviors, which we grouped into six categories (or "traits"), all of which are equally important and mutually reinforcing.[3] We then built a 360-degree assessment tool for use by followers to rate the presence of these traits among leaders. The tool has now been used by over 3,500 raters to evaluate over 450 leaders. The results are illuminating.

These are the six traits or behaviors that we found distinguish inclusive leaders from others:[4]

> *Visible commitment:* They articulate authentic commitment to diversity, challenge the status quo, hold others accountable and make diversity and inclusion a personal priority.

> *Humility:* They are modest about capabilities, admit mistakes, and create the space for others to contribute.

> *Awareness of bias:* They show awareness of personal blind spots as well as flaws in the system and work hard to ensure meritocracy.

> *Curiosity about others:* They demonstrate an open mindset and deep curiosity about others, listen without judgment,

and seek with empathy to understand those around them.

Cultural intelligence: They are attentive to others' cultures and adapt as required.

Effective collaboration: They empower others, pay attention to diversity of thinking and psychological safety, and focus on team cohesion.

These traits may seem like the obvious ones, similar to those that are broadly important for good leadership. But the difference between assessing and developing good leadership generally versus inclusive leadership in particular lies in three specific insights.

First, most leaders in the study were unsure about whether others experienced them as inclusive or not. More particularly, only a third (36%) saw their inclusive-leadership capabilities as others did, another third (32%) overrated their capabilities, and the final third (33%) underrated their capabilities.

Even more importantly, rarely were leaders certain about the specific behaviors that actually have an impact on being rated as more or less inclusive.

Second, being rated as an inclusive leader is not determined by *averaging* all members' scores but rather by the *distribution* of raters' scores. For example, it's not enough that, on average, raters agree that a leader "approaches diversity and inclusiveness wholeheartedly." Using a five-point scale (ranging from "strongly agree" to "strongly disagree"), an average rating could mean that some team members disagree while others agree. To be an inclusive leader, one must ensure that *everyone* agrees or strongly agrees that they are being treated fairly and respectfully, are valued, and have a sense of belonging and are psychologically safe.

Third, inclusive leadership is not about occasional grand gestures, but regular, smaller-scale comments and actions. By comparing the qualitative feedback regarding the most inclusive (top 25%) and the least inclusive (bottom 25%) of leaders in our sample, we discovered that inclusive leadership is tangible and practiced every day.

These verbatim responses from our assessments illustrate some of the tangible behaviors of the most inclusive leaders in the study:

- *Shares personal weaknesses:* "[This leader] will openly ask about information that she is not aware of. She demonstrates a humble unpretentious work manner. This puts others at ease, enabling them to speak out and voice their opinions, which she values."

- *Learns about cultural differences:* "[This leader] has taken the time to learn the ropes (common words, idioms, customs, likes/dislikes) and the cultural pillars."

- *Acknowledges team members as individuals:* "[This leader] leads a team of over 100 people and yet addresses every team member by name and knows the work stream that they support and the work that they do."

The following verbatims illustrate some of the behaviors of the least inclusive leaders:

- *Overpowers others:* "He can be very direct and overpowering which limits the ability of those around him to contribute to meetings or participate in conversations."

- *Displays favoritism:* "Work is assigned to the same top performers, creating unsustainable workloads. [There is a] need to give newer team members opportunities to prove themselves."

- *Discounts alternative views:* "[This leader] can have very set ideas on specific topics. Sometimes it is difficult to get an alternative view across. There is a risk that his team may hold back from bringing forward challenging and alternative points of view."

What leaders say and do has an outsized impact on others, but our research indicates that this effect is even more pronounced when they are leading diverse teams. Subtle words and acts of exclusion by leaders, or overlooking the exclusive behaviors of others, easily reinforces the status quo. It takes energy and deliberate effort to create an inclusive culture, and that starts with leaders paying much more attention to what they say and do on a daily basis and making adjustments as necessary.

Here are four ways for leaders to get started:

- *Know your inclusive-leadership shadow:* Seek feedback on whether you are perceived as inclusive, especially from people who are different from you. This will help you to see your blind spots, strengths, and development areas. It will also signal that diversity and inclusion are important to you. Scheduling regular check-ins with members of your team to ask how you can make them feel more included also sends the message.

- *Be visible and vocal:* Tell a compelling and explicit narrative about why being inclusive is important to you personally and the business more broadly. For example, share your personal stories at public forums and conferences.

- *Deliberately seek out difference:* Give people on the periphery of your network the chance to speak up, invite different people to the table, and catch up with a broader network. For example, seek out opportunities to work with cross-functional or multidisciplinary teams to leverage diverse strengths.

- *Check your impact:* Look for signals that you are having a positive impact. Are people copying your role modeling? Is a more diverse group of people sharing ideas with you? Are people working together more collaboratively? Ask a trusted adviser to give you candid feedback on the areas you have been working on.

There's more to be learned about how to become an inclusive leader and harness the power of diverse teams, but one thing is clear: Leaders who consciously practice inclusive leadership and actively develop their capability will see the results in the superior performance of their diverse teams.

JULIET BOURKE is a professor of practice in the School of Management and Governance, UNSW Business School, University of New South Wales, and a workplace consultant. She is the author of *Which Two Heads Are Better Than One: The Extraordinary Power of Diversity of Thinking and Inclusive Leadership.* ANDREA TITUS is an organizational psychologist, executive manager at Westpac Banking Corporation, and vice president of SIOPA.

Notes

1. Juliet Bourke, "The Diversity and Inclusion Revolution: Eight Powerful Truths," *Deloitte Review* 22 (2018), https://

www2.deloitte.com/us/en/insights/deloitte-review/
issue-22/diversity-and-inclusion-at-work-eight-powerful
-truths.html.

2. Deloitte Australia and the Victorian Equal Opportunity
and Human Rights Commission, "Waiter, Is That Inclusion in My Soup? A New Recipe to Improve Business Performance," May 2013, https://www2.deloitte.com/content/
dam/Deloitte/au/Documents/human-capital/deloitte-au
-hc-diversity-inclusion-soup-0513.pdf.

3. Bernadette Dillon and Juliet Bourke, "The Six Signa-
ture Traits of Inclusive Leadership," Deloitte University
Press, 2016, https://www2.deloitte.com/content/dam/
Deloitte/au/Documents/human-capital/deloitte-au-hc-six
-signature-traits-inclusive-leadership-020516.pdf.

4. Juliet Bourke and Andrea Titus, "The Key to Inclusive
Leadership," hbr.org, March 6, 2020, https://hbr.org
/2020/03/the-key-to-inclusive-leadership.

Adapted from "Why Inclusive Leaders Are Good for Organizations,
and How to Become One" on hbr.org, March 29, 2019
(product #H04V8Y).

2

The Value of Belonging at Work

By Evan W. Carr, Andrew Reece,
Gabriella Rosen Kellerman, and Alexi Robichaux

Social belonging is a fundamental human need, hardwired into our DNA. And yet, 40% of people say that they feel isolated at work, and the result has been lower organizational commitment and engagement. In a nutshell, companies are blowing it. U.S. businesses spend nearly $8 billion each year on diversity and inclusion (D&I) trainings that miss the mark because they neglect our need to feel included.

From this 10,000-foot perspective, the costs associated with this drought of workplace belonging are eye-catching. Zooming in a bit helps focus on the reality of the problem. Exclusion is damaging because it actually hurts: The sensation is akin to physical pain. And it's a sting we've all experienced at one time or another. To feel left out is a deeply human problem, which is why its consequences carry such heft and why its causes are so hard to root out of even the healthiest workplaces.

Humans are so fundamentally social that we can even bond with strangers over the very experience of not having anyone with whom to bond. Consider this story in the *Guardian*, which prompted people to share their own experiences of feeling left out at work. More than 800 wrote in.[1] One anonymous worker in the United Kingdom lamented, "I get paid well to do something I enjoy, and . . . [I'm] surrounded by clever, funny, like-minded people. And for 45 or 50 hours every week, I feel isolated."

To better understand this basic need to *belong*— a key missing ingredient in the D&I conversation— BetterUp conducted research to investigate the role of belonging at work and the outsized consequences of its absence.[2] For this project, defining belonging became our first and, in some ways, trickiest task. Our data showed that belonging is a close cousin to many related experiences: mattering, identification, and social connection. The unifying thread across these themes is that they all revolve around the sense of being accepted and included by those around you. We set out to study how that develops—or doesn't—in the workplace, what it means for employees and organizations, and whether it's possible to turn a bad situation around.

The research is novel in two ways: First, it quantifies the value of workplace belonging, both with correlational and experimental findings. Second, it offers new, evidence-based interventions to boost inclusion. Following earlier BetterUp studies on loneliness and purpose, we first surveyed 1,789 full-time U.S. employees across many industries and then conducted a series of experiments with more than 2,000 live participants to observe and measure the costs of exclusion. Here's what we found.

Belonging is good for business

If workers feel like they belong, companies reap substantial bottom-line benefits. High belonging was linked to a whopping 56% increase in job performance, a 50% drop in turnover risk, and a 75% reduction in sick days. For a 10,000-person company, this would result in annual savings of more than $52 million.

Employees with higher workplace belonging also showed a 167% increase in their employer promoter score (their willingness to recommend their company to others). They also received double the raises and 18 times more promotions.

Exclusion leads to team (and self-) sabotage

Our survey findings reveal workplace exclusion as a systemic issue that generates hefty financial losses. But does exclusion actually *cause* measurable hits to team performance?

To address this question, we conducted a series of experiments. Initially, workers were assigned to a team with two other "participants" (bots programmed to act like teammates), using a collaborative virtual ball-toss game.[3] *Included* workers had teammates that consistently threw them the ball, whereas *excluded* workers only got the ball a couple of times. After this, participants completed a simple task where they could earn money either for themselves or for their entire team. The longer participants persisted in the task, the more money they earned.

What differences did we see between the excluded and included teammates? When participants were told the payouts would be shared with the team, the excluded people worked less hard than the included ones, even though it meant sacrificing earnings. When participants were told the payouts would benefit them and them alone, excluded team members worked just as much as included ones. We replicated this effect again and again, across four separate studies. We can now say that feeling excluded *causes* us to give less effort to the team.

The harmful effects of exclusion can be reversed

These findings invite the question: Can exclusion be *fixed*? Many solutions have been proposed, but few are based in experimental evidence.

As such, a new round of our experiments tested three interventions, each designed to mitigate the costs of exclusion:

1. *Gaining perspective:* Previous participants shared reflections with current participants on their exclusion experience and how they coped.

2. *Encouraging mentorship:* Participants imagined how they would coach someone else through exclusion.

3. *Finding empowerment:* Participants planned out how they would restructure this team experience to make it more inclusive and enjoyable.

All three interventions succeeded in causing excluded team members to behave more like included ones. Notably, the mentorship and empowerment tools were so powerful that those excluded participants worked *even harder* for their team than their included peers.

Having an ally protects workers from exclusion

It might be difficult to identify exclusion on the spot as it's happening, so another valuable intervention strategy would be to buffer workers against the negative effects of exclusion in the first place. One possibility is that having an *ally* might take the sting out of being excluded by other team members.

We tested this in another experiment, wherein an ally bot was programmed to signal inclusion by throwing the ball to the participant, while the other bots ignored them. Importantly, the ally only threw the ball to the participant as much as anyone else did; that is, the ally offered equal (not special) treatment. We found that having one fair-acting ally made people more willing to work for their entire team, protecting group performance from the negative effects of exclusion.

How do we create a workplace of belonging?

Our research demonstrates clear, actionable paths forward to help resolve the epidemic of workplace exclusion. Even the most effective recruiting strategy for diversity won't lead to long-term change if new talent isn't supported to succeed. Fortunately, our findings show that we are not powerless in the face of exclusion.

Individuals coping with left-out feelings can adapt these new evidence-based tools of gaining perspective from others, mentoring those in a similar condition, and thinking of strategies for improving the situation. For team leaders and colleagues who want to help others feel included, our research suggests that serving as a fair-minded ally—someone who treats everyone equally—can offer protection to buffer the exclusionary behavior of others. They can also share stories about how they have coped with similar challenges and see what suggestions teammates have for improving the situation. These strategies would help workers not only navigate tricky workplace dynamics, but also drive their own version of change, especially when the system isn't working for everyone. Leaders and organizations should invite employee feedback and take it seriously; this behavior is a cornerstone of inclusive companies. Workers need to feel like they belong to something they value—and that they have the power to bring about change when it's needed.

EVAN W. CARR is a senior research scientist at Amazon Web Services and was previously a quantitative behavioral scientist at BetterUp. ANDREW REECE is a behavioral data scientist at BetterUp. GABRIELLA ROSEN KELLERMAN is the chief innovation officer at BetterUp and head of BetterUp Labs. ALEXI ROBICHAUX is cofounder and CEO of BetterUp.

Notes

1. Sarah Marsh, "'You Are Not the Only Lonely Worker': Our Readers on Making Friends at Work," *Guardian*, February 2, 2016, https://www.theguardian.com/lifeandstyle/2016/feb/02/you-are-not-the-only-lonely-worker-our-readers-on-making-friends-at-work.
2. Gabriella Rosen Kellerman and Andrew Reece, "The Value of Belonging at Work: Investing in Workplace Inclusion," BetterUp.com, https://grow.betterup.com/resources/the-value-of-belonging-at-work-the-business-case-for-investing-in-workplace-inclusion-event.
3. Kipling D. Williams and Blair Jarvis, "Cyberball: A Program for Use in Research on Interpersonal Ostracism and Acceptance," *Behavior Research Methods* 38, no. 1 (2006): 174–180.

Adapted from content posted on hbr.org, December 16, 2019 (product #H05BT9).

3

Make Psychological Safety a Strategic Priority

By Maren Gube and Debra Sabatini Hennelly

The Covid-19 pandemic, geopolitical instability, and unpredictable markets have made organizational resilience like food in the desert: critical for survival but challenging to grow. By making resilience a strategic priority, leaders ensure that their organizations can stretch and adapt.

Much has been written about psychological safety's role in improving workplace wellness. But to weather uncertainty, organizations also need to make psychological safety a strategic priority, creating a culture where employees can comfortably raise concerns, contribute ideas, and share unique perspectives.

Three cultural dimensions are critical for resilience:

- *Integrity:* Ethical leadership and courageous candor

- *Innovation:* Fearless collaborative creativity

- *Inclusion:* Authentic respect and belonging

These sustain business continuity, competitiveness, and growth—the intersection of these three dimensions forms the core of a psychologically safe culture. To strengthen resilience, leaders must understand how to connect these three siloed dimensions of culture and develop leadership attributes that encourage candor.

In what follows, we explain why psychological safety is necessary for the highest expression of integrity, innovation, and inclusion; explore the obstacles to investing in psychological safety; and illustrate how senior leaders can overcome these obstacles to boost resilience.

Psychological safety as the foundation of resilience

The simple business case for each dimension of resilience is well known. Ethical business behavior (integrity) enhances financial performance, employees who generate and share more ideas improve profitability through innovation, and organizational diversity predicts higher financial returns (inclusion). Both integrity and inclusion are key elements of assessing an organization's environment, sustainability, and governance (ESG) commitments and performance.

Beyond their direct impacts on the bottom line, the three dimensions share an intrinsic connection: Psychological safety is at their core, and any breach erodes their foundation. The fear of retaliation for speaking up compromises integrity, curbing creative ideation leads to stagnation, and disrespectful interactions have a disproportionately toxic impact on engagement and belonging.

Psychological safety does not happen automatically. Because our brains are hardwired to keep us safe, our default mode is to presume some level of threat in most environments. Like animals that sense a predator in the forest, humans tend to stay quiet in a workplace form of "freeze" (from the "fight, flight, freeze" reaction) unless we know we can safely speak up with concerns, fresh ideas, or unique perspectives.

When leaders recognize the connections between psychological safety and resilience, they can model the behaviors that welcome candor—and set expectations throughout the organization to enhance integrity, innovation, and inclusion.

Dimension #1: Integrity

Organizations with a culture of integrity don't sacrifice doing the right thing for short-term profit. Leaders trust employees to challenge myopic directives, and they empower team members to own decisions that safeguard long-term resilience. Candor is expected, as well as protected, to prevent (or detect and address) legal or ethical issues that could derail or shut down the business.

Two key reasons employees refrain from speaking up are fear of retaliation and a perception that even well-founded concerns will not be addressed. When leaders are committed to encouraging candor, they can be intentional about changing these perceptions.

Early warning signals prevent problems from spiraling out of control. In the last two years, 55% of all tips about workplace fraud came from employees.[1] The sooner tips are investigated, the sooner an organization can mitigate related losses. When employees at all levels feel safe to raise concerns, problem behaviors like bullying and harassment can also be confronted in a timely manner.

Retaliation for speaking up about wrongdoing is at an all-time high. The contradiction is not lost on employees, whose companies' codes of conduct oblige them to speak up. Yet, these "upstanders" often face overt or subtle retribution if they do.

Employees who don't have safe internal channels for reporting issues sometimes choose to blow the whistle with the government or the media. Despite the risk of stigma, some find that they have no other alternative. However, external reporting threatens the resilience of organizations in multiple ways. Perhaps the greatest risk comes from the missed opportunity to address the problem in house, early, before the damage escalates.

Dimension #2: Innovation

In a rapidly changing world, continual product and process innovation are necessary elements of sustainable organizational performance. However, the stress of uncertainty reduces individual creativity and diminishes the drive to explore and challenge existing paradigms.

Innovation tends to decline when external risk increases. Focusing on psychological safety internally helps counter that tendency. Embracing "what if . . ." questions fosters a culture of curiosity for generating possible solutions.

The innovation imperative sometimes gets misconstrued as a drive to innovate at any cost. Dissenters can be marginalized and overruled in a new product push, to the detriment of the organization. Putting the brakes on a train that is just about to leave the station requires psychological safety—and is unlikely to happen unless leaders are on board with encouraging passionate dialogue.

Dimension #3: Inclusion

Engagement and belonging are grounded in inclusion. They are foundational to the resilience of not only the organization, but also individual employees. In 2021, two-thirds of people who left their jobs said they did so because they did not feel included, valued, respected, trusted, or cared for.[2] Almost half of U.S. employees were looking for other opportunities, and the number of women intending to leave was startling. Underrepresented (and sought-after) groups were particularly likely to be on the move.[3]

Diversity among employees helps companies anticipate, cope with, and adapt to risk and turbulent conditions. For example, the International Monetary Fund has cited "a high degree of groupthink" (that is, a lack of diverse viewpoints) as a contributing factor for failing to sound alarms about the impending financial crisis in 2007.[4]

Diverse teams have a broader knowledge base, which allows for better environmental scanning and risk analysis, especially in complex environments. Experiential diversity among team members increases the range of potential coping strategies and leads to better decision making under threat. The question "What am I not seeing?" is more likely to surface rich perspectives, latent concerns, and novel suggestions when the team is diverse—and when all voices are heard thanks to psychological safety.

Obstacles to psychological safety

Given the multidimensional benefits of psychological safety, why is it so challenging to make it a strategic priority? Be aware of these two primary obstacles.

Obstacle #1: Blind spots

Senior leaders may not be connecting the dots across functional silos in the organization, overlooking the opportunities to work together. For example, functional professionals (for example, legal, risk management, R&D, HR) tend to focus their requests for limited internal resources vertically in the hierarchy. By competing for support for one-off initiatives—rather than collaborating—they miss the opportunity to help senior leaders realize the cross-functional alchemy of investing in psychological safety.

The onus is on senior leaders to see beyond functions as individual cost centers. By identifying opportunities to champion psychological safety across previously disparate initiatives, they optimize resources for a multidimensional return on investment that enables all voices to be heard.

Obstacle #2: Vulnerability

Psychological safety demands modes of decision making that are different from what many leaders are used to. It requires leadership attributes like accessibility, humility, and empathy.

One of the most valuable actions leaders in resilient organizations take is to set their personal agendas aside. Many leaders are fearful of feedback that may leave them vulnerable to criticism, but transparent decision making gets beyond seeing only what we want to see. Input that contradicts our subjective perceptions can be hard to hear, but often provides valuable signals for course correcting.

Gustavo Razzetti, culture designer and author of the book *Remote, Not Distant*, points out that all too often, leaders claim to have an open agenda and welcome dissent—and yet, out-of-the-box ideas and candid feedback are quickly shut down when leaders become defensive. "Even brilliant leaders can have a hard time accepting change, like Steve Jobs when the idea of the iPhone was first floated," Razzetti says.[5] "[W]e need to stop thinking of them as superheroes with all the answers."

Taking the lead on psychological safety

Like trust, psychological safety takes a long time to build—and even longer to rebuild once breached. Here are five focus areas for leaders who want to make psychological safety a strategic priority in the service of organizational resilience.

1. *Ask questions about the culture.* Periodically conduct assessments of engagement, integrity, and other aspects of culture. Pay attention to the results and how they change over time. Take the time to map out existing and desired cultures and design a road map for necessary transformations.

2. *Be clear about your expectations for ethical decision making and integrity.* Silence and ambiguity have consequences. Be intentional about seeking out early warning signals—and clear about responding. Prohibit retaliation

against "upstanders" and ensure that employees always have a safe channel for raising concerns and that they know how to access it. Build trust by extending trust. Align your actions with your words and show your own vulnerabilities first.

3. *Encourage outside-the-box thinking.* Perceived leader support influences creative performance and innovation. Reframe and celebrate mistakes as organizational learning opportunities. Encourage employees to generate and share ideas, which need not always be polished. Welcome dissent without judgment. Assign and rotate the role of "challenger" at meetings.

4. *Invest in and personally support your diversity, equity, and inclusion (DEI) initiatives.* Having even one ally in the workplace fosters a sense of belonging and can encourage people to speak up—be that ally. Use your relative

privilege to share, rather than hoard, power. Foster diversity and inclusion as explicit business strategies, include them in your ESG-related commitments, and tie them to executive compensation. Know how to avoid the pitfalls of disrespectful, noninclusive cultures that make for toxic workplaces with high turnover. Prioritize clear communications, assign projects and roles based on strengths, foster relationships, and invite people to be part of the decision making.

5. *Build accountability for psychological safety into performance metrics.* Set relevant objectives and provide the necessary training for your managers so that psychological safety rises to the level of a strategic objective rather than a "nice-to-have." Emphasize leadership skills around emotional and social intelligence in career development and promotions. Take the metrics seriously and hold people accountable.

Also, hold yourself accountable by asking yourself: How am I modeling these behaviors? How can I set up my direct reports to be successful?

Learning to be nimble and resilient in the new world of work requires an uncommon level of human connection. Understanding how integrity, innovation, and inclusion are connected—and sparking that alchemy—helps organizational leaders move beyond their blind spots and *own* psychological safety as a strategic imperative. These three cultural dimensions can map the route to resilience and sustain an abundant harvest, no matter how unpredictable the terrain ahead.

MAREN GUBE guides organizations pursuing cultures of fearless collaborative creativity through her research and professional practice. She helps leaders develop the necessary emotional literacy for adapting to change and disruption. Maren empowers teams to unravel invisible systemic threats, decoding the contextual social emotions that subconsciously drive organizational culture. Her blend of executive experience and PhD inquiry brings new perspectives to leaders. Her award-winning work on creativity and why women leave STEM fields has earned citations on both sides of the Atlantic. She is the coauthor of the article "4 Ways to Spark Creativity When You're Feeling Stressed" on hbr.org and executive director of Resiliti. Read more about her at marengube.com. **DEBRA SABATINI HENNELLY** advises executives and boards on enhancing organizational resilience by creating cultures of candor, inclusion, integrity, and innovation. She engages teams and leaders directly to identify and address obstacles to psychological safety and ethical decision-making, increasing collaboration, wellbeing, and productivity. Debbie also coaches ethics and compliance professionals in effective leadership and personal resilience. Her pragmatic approach is informed by her engineering and legal background and decades of corporate leadership, C-suite, and advisory roles in compliance and ethics, legal, environment and safety, and strategic management. Debbie is an adjunct professor in Fordham University Law School's Program on Corporate Ethics & Compliance, a frequent speaker at professional conferences, and the founder and president of Resiliti (resiliti.com).

Notes

1. Association of Certified Fraud Examiners, "Occupational Fraud 2022: A Report to the Nations," https://acfepublic

.s3.us-west-2.amazonaws.com/2022+Report+to+the+Na tions.pdf.

2. Mark C. Crowley, "It's Not Just Money. This Is What's Still Driving the Great Resignation," FastCompany.com, March 5, 2022, https://www.fastcompany.com/90727646/its-not-just -money-this-is-whats-still-driving-the-great-resignation.

3. David Rice, "Stemming the Tide: How to Retain Diverse Employees in the Great Resignation," DiversityIncBest Practices.com, https://www.diversityincbestpractices.com/ stemming-the-tide-how-to-retain-diverse-employees-in -the-great-resignation/.

4. International Monetary Fund Independent Evaluation Office, "Why Did the IMF Fail to Give Clear Warning?," in *IMF Performance in the Run-Up to the Financial and Economic Crisis* (Washington, DC: IMF, 2011).

5. Zameena Mejia, "Steve Jobs Almost Prevented the Apple iPhone from Being Invented," CNBC Make It, September 12, 2017, https://www.cnbc.com/2017/09/12/why -steve-jobs-almost-prevented-the-apple-iphone-from -being-invented.html.

Adapted from "Resilient Organizations Make Psychological Safety a Strategic Priority" on hbr.org, August 25, 2022 (product #H0771Y).

4

The Importance of Being an Inclusive Colleague

By Juliet Bourke

Already a hot topic, creating an inclusive workplace has become even more critical for organizations seeking to attract and retain talent, and enhance productivity. Historically, companies have focused on putting in place organizational diversity policies. More recently the focus has shifted to inclusive leadership and the powerful role played by leaders in setting the tone, modeling inclusive behaviors, and calling people to account. Both of these strategies are critical, but they overlook the significance of peer relationships.

There's a good reason for that. In academic literature as well as industry practice, inclusion has been conceptualized as a psychosocial experience between an individual and a group.[1] In other words, *only* a group (or a leader as representative of a group) has the power to make an individual feel fairly treated, valued, respected, and connected. But is that really right?

Over the last few years I've been investigating the impact of peer relationships on an individual's experience of inclusion. My first study involved deep-dive interviews with 21 diverse employees working in different project teams in a global firm. In a second ethnographic study, I observed the regular meetings of a project team (comprising people of different nationalities, technical capabilities, and gender) over a period of two months to see if (and how) inclusive behaviors between peers manifested themselves in practice. In other words, I took out a microscope to explore people's granular experiences, and then zoomed back out to make sense of the relationship between small acts of inclusion or exclusion, an individual's job performance, and team effectiveness more broadly. Here's what I learned.

Interpersonal inclusion is manifested by and developed through three sets of behaviors

The interviewees from my first study told me in no uncertain terms that peers absolutely have the power to include or exclude, and the exercise of that power makes a meaningful difference to work performance. Further, both studies identified that peer inclusion is demonstrated through three different types of behaviors.

1. Helping each other out. These behaviors, which I call "instrumental assistance," are those that help a peer to perform their work tasks, such as by providing information, making introductions to contacts, giving endorsements in meetings, and offering advice.

What's significant about these actions is that they are discretionary and fall outside the strict ambit of one's job description. For example, one senior manager told me of a peer who came out of a meeting and quickly gave him a heads-up on what was covered rather than waiting until the end of the week and the formal project status report.

During my observations, I often saw peers subtly endorse and amplify each other (for example, "As Pedro said . . . "), thus helping to underscore a peer's point and increasing their potential influence over proceedings. This particular behavior is reminiscent of a technique reportedly used by President Obama's female staffers to reinforce and amplify points made by their female peers.

2. Taking emotional care of others. This refers to the care, support, and personal interest people demonstrate toward their peers, which helps to develop emotional bonds. Interviewees spoke about social-

izing with their peers, joking, and banter, as well as providing space for venting and showing an authentic interest in a peer's personal life (for example, children, pets, or sport). One junior employee told me about how he and his peer started each day with "some kind of little joke," while many others talked about taking a quick break from the office environment to have a coffee together. Of course, with the rise of hybrid work, in-person socializing occurs less frequently, but that was countered by an observable increase in the practice of checking in with peers at a more personal level at the beginning or end of online meetings.

3. Making physical connections. The third behavior, which I call "embodied connection," refers to the ways in which team members use their physical beings to create and communicate a closer connection through body language and the sharing of space. For example, interviewees talked about walking together

to meetings, deliberately sitting next to each other, or if a meeting was virtual, sharing their personal backgrounds rather than using an impersonal corporate photo, and exaggerating positive nonverbal cues such as smiling and nodding.

What's clear about these examples is that each involved a pint-sized effort. Nevertheless, the impact was profound psychosocially in terms of feeling included, especially when these micro acts of interpersonal inclusion accumulated over time.

Interpersonal inclusion is a reciprocal process and is highly beneficial to individual job performance and team effectiveness

The benefit of interpersonal inclusion between peers is not just psychological; it also has very practical consequences in terms of boosting individual job performance and improving team effectiveness, according to all of the interviewees. Why? Because each act of interpersonal inclusion is essentially a trade of valuable resources. It might be a direct trade (that is, I give you an act of instrumental assistance and you give me one back) or a diffuse trade (that is, if I give you the space to vent, I'm building a more supportive culture that will be there for me should I need it). This makes interpersonal inclusion sound a bit calculating, and interviewees were at pains to play down that connotation. They preferred to think of interpersonal inclusion in terms of helping a peer rather than "cashing in favors." Nevertheless, the reality was that each trade strengthened a peer's sense of inclusivity (that is, my peer cares about me) and provided the practical instrumental and emotional resources needed to do a job.

Importantly, given that interpersonal inclusion is a reciprocal process, anyone can kick-start it. This challenges the traditional conceptualization of inclusion as, by nature, a passive experience, with a person waiting for an act of inclusion to be extended toward them by the dominant group or the leader. It turns out that inclusion can be either a passive *or* an active experience, with half of the interviewees saying that they actively included others as a strategy to make themselves feel more included. Further, they did this by using one or more of the three behaviors of inter-personal inclusion to trigger a reciprocal response. Of course, it didn't always work, but it did tip the odds in their favor. This is a very empowering message.

So what does this all add up to? Interviewees told me that these small behaviors have an outsized im-pact on motivation and energy ("If you feel included, you want to come to work every day; you feel more motivated," as one told me) as well as psychological safety and thus the flow of information and speed of problem-solving (thereby reducing the duplication of effort). Such acts also facilitate deeper insight into a peer's skills and thus better job-matching, as well as helping employees to grow and develop on the job. In sum, interpersonal inclusion between peers helps with retention and growing the quality of employees' human capital, thus contributing to team effectiveness more broadly.

On the flip side: Interpersonal exclusion is damaging and usually subtle

But it's not all roses. Interviewees described interpersonal exclusion to me as the antithesis of interpersonal inclusion, albeit that it was more likely to be manifested as an omission than commission. In other words, interpersonal exclusion was often experienced through a failure to provide instrumental assistance, emotional bond, or embodied connection rather than via an overt act, such as a snide comment.

For example, I observed people consistently give endorsements to some peers but not others (and this was not driven by the peer's deservedness). I heard about overtures to lunch that were ignored, and I saw people respond impassively to ideas presented by some but animatedly to those presented by others (once again, irrespective of the quality of the idea).

Given that these acts were omissions and small in scale, they were difficult for the excluded peer to put their finger on and name for what they were. Nevertheless, the effects were profound in terms of diminishing motivation and energy, constricting channels of communication, and causing people to hold back their discretionary effort.

Disappointingly, in both phases of my research I saw that those who identified themselves as more different to the group than similar were three times as likely to report, and experience, acts of interpersonal exclusion than those who were similar. Some of these acts seemed deliberate, but many more of them appeared to be unconscious. People seemed unaware of the differences in their behavior toward different peers, and they also underestimated the impact of their small acts of interpersonal exclusion on their peer, in terms of both job performance and their own team's effectiveness. In essence, they failed to recognize or give weight to the fact that interpersonal exclusion is a self-defeating behavior, because it restricts access to a larger pool of resources and creates a more transactional workplace culture.

If an organization's objective is to create an inclusive culture, and thus attract and retain talent, this research reveals the significance of focusing on (horizontal) peer relationships. As such, it complements organizational diversity policies and (vertical) inclusive leadership practices. Moreover, it offers practical insights about how to do this by identifying the nature of interpersonal inclusion, thus making it easier for people to consciously and equitably demonstrate these behaviors with their peers.

In sum, paying much more attention to these small acts of instrumental assistance, emotional bond, and embodied connection can make a world of difference, especially given that in increasingly flat hierarchies "co-workers are not only a vital part of the social environment at work; they can literally define it," as Dan Chiaburu and David Harrison have written.[2] In other words, it is peers who help define what is means to work in an inclusive workplace, and thus, in concert with organizational policies and inclusive leaders, encouraging more inclusive relationships between peers can help teams to be more effective and organizations to achieve their aspirations.

JULIET BOURKE is a professor of practice in the School of Management and Governance, UNSW Business School, University of New South Wales, and a workplace consultant. She is the author of *Which Two Heads Are Better Than One: The Extraordinary Power of Diversity of Thinking and Inclusive Leadership*.

Notes

1. Wiebren S. Jansen et al., "Inclusion: Conceptualization and Measurement," *European Journal of Social Psychology* 44, no. 4 (2014): 370–385.
2. Dan S. Chiaburu and David A. Harrison, "Do Peers Make the Place? Conceptual Synthesis and Meta-analysis of

Coworker Effects on Perceptions, Attitudes, OCBs, and Performance," *Journal of Applied Psychology* 93, no. 5 (2008): 1082–1103.

Adapted from "3 Small Ways to Be a More Inclusive Colleague" on hbr.org, December 13, 2021 (product #H06Q9C).

5

Recognizing and Responding to Microaggressions

By Ella F. Washington

We've all been in situations at work when someone says or does something that feels hostile or offensive to some aspect of our identity—and the person doesn't even realize it. These kinds of actions—insensitive statements, questions, or assumptions—are called "microaggressions," and they can target many aspects of who we are. For example, they could be related to someone's race, gender, sexuality, parental status, socioeconomic background, mental health, or any other aspect of our identity.

Most often, microaggressions are aimed at traditionally marginalized identity groups. Yet these hurtful actions can happen to anyone, of any background, at any professional level. A microaggression against a Black woman, for example, could be "You aren't like the other Black people I know" (indicating the person is different from the stereotypes of Black people), whereas one for a white male might be, "Oh, you don't ever have to worry about fitting in" (indicating that all white men are always comfortable and accepted). Essentially, microaggressions are based on a simple, damaging idea: "Because you are X, you probably are/are not or like/don't like Y."

One criticism of discourse about microaggressions is that our society has become "hypersensitive" and that casual remarks are now blown out of proportion. However, research is clear about the impact seemingly innocuous statements can have on one's physical and mental health, especially over the course of an entire career: increased rates of depression, prolonged stress and trauma, physical concerns like headaches, high blood pressure, and difficulties with sleep.[1] Microaggressions can negatively impact careers as they are related to increased burnout and less job satisfaction and require significant cognitive and emotional resources to recover from them. Employers are now paying closer attention to how organizational culture can influence whether or not employees want to leave. One study found that 7 in 10 workers said they would be upset by a microaggression, and half said the action would make them consider leaving their job.

So the reality is that microaggressions are not so micro in terms of their impact. They should be taken seriously, because at their core they signal disrespect and reflect inequality.

To create inclusive, welcoming, and healthy workplaces, we must actively combat microaggressions. Doing so requires understanding how they show up and how to respond productively to them, whether they happen to us or to colleagues. Inclusive work environments are not just nice to have—they positively contribute to employee well-being and mental and physical health.

Building inclusive workplaces requires candid, authentic conversations on tough subjects, like sexism, homophobia, and racism—and it's natural to worry that we may commit microaggressions in these kinds of conversations by saying the wrong thing. The more awareness we have about how microaggressions show up, the more we can work toward decreasing them in the workplace. Yet the reality is that we all make mistakes, so you should know what to do if you witness a microaggression or commit one.

As I share in my book, *The Necessary Journey*, awareness is always the first step. Here are some ways to become more aware of microaggressions, interrupt them when we see them, and promote workplace cultures with fewer microaggressions.

Being more aware of microaggressions

There are many words and phrases in the English language that are rooted in systemically favoring dominant groups in society. Thus many parts of our everyday speech have historical roots in racism, sexism, and other forms of discrimination. For example, the following terms you may casually hear in the workplace have hurtful connotations:

- "Blacklist" refers to a list of things that are seen negatively, juxtaposed against "whitelist," a list of things that are seen positively.

- "Man up" equates gender with strength or competence.

- "Peanut gallery" originated in the 1800s and referred to the sections of segregated theaters usually occupied by Black people.

These words and phrases can trigger thoughts of current and past discrimination for people. Taking time to be intentional with the language you use is a significant part of treating each other with respect. While it's unrealistic to know every cultural minefield that may exist in language, the goal is to be thoughtful about the origins of common phrases and, more importantly, to change your use of these terms if you become aware that they are problematic. For example, if you are looking to encourage someone, telling them to "rise to the moment" or "be brave" is a better way to communicate the sentiment than "man up." It takes work to unlearn the many fraught words and phrases in our cultural lexicon, but most people find it's not that difficult to do once they set their minds to actively being more inclusive.

Here are examples of a few types of microaggressions that you may hear within and outside the workplace:

- Race/ethnicity

  - "I didn't realize you were Jewish—you don't look Jewish," signaling that a person of the Jewish heritage has a stereotypical look. (Of course, similar statements happen to people from many backgrounds.)

  - "I believe the most qualified person should get the job," signaling that someone is being given an unfair advantage because of their race.

- Citizenship

  - "Your English is so good—where are your parents from?" signaling that people with English as a second language are generally less capable of speaking English.

  - "But where are you *really* from?" signaling that where someone grew up isn't their "true" origin. This microaggression often happens to people who are in ethnic and racial minorities, whom others assume are immigrants.

- Class

  - "How did you get into that school?" signaling that someone's background makes them an anomaly at a prestigious school.

  - "You don't seem like you grew up poor," signaling that someone from a particular socioeconomic background should look or behave a certain way.

- Mental health

  - "That's insane" or "That's crazy," using terminology related to a mental health condition to describe surprise or astonishment.

  - "You don't seem like you are depressed. Sometimes I get sad too," minimizing the experiences of people with mental illness.

- "Don't mind my OCD!" using the acronym for obsessive compulsive disorder, a mental health condition where an individual is plagued by obsessive thoughts and fears that can lead to compulsions, to describe attention to detail, fastidiousness, or being organized.

- Gender

  - "Don't be so sensitive," signaling that someone, likely a woman, is being "too emotional" in a situation where a man would be more objective.

  - "Thanks, sweetheart" and similar comments often directed at women, which are often not appreciated or even offensive.

- Sexuality

  - "That's so gay" to mean something is bad or undesirable, signaling that being gay is associated with negative and undesirable characteristics.

– "Do you have a wife/husband?" which assumes heteronormative culture and behaviors, versus more inclusive phrasing such as "Do you have a partner?"

- Parental status

– "You don't have kids to pick up, so you can work later, right?" signaling that someone without children does not have a life outside of work.

In the workplace, microaggressions can happen in all types of conversations. For example, they may occur during hiring when someone is evaluating a candidate with a different demographic background than their own, during the performance evaluation process when someone is highlighting the positive or negative aspects of an employee, or in customer service when someone is interacting with customers who have a different first language than their own. We should all become more aware of microaggressions in general, but in professional environments, there should be a special level of attention to and care taken in the language we use.

Responding to microaggressions

The more you increase your awareness of microaggressions, the more you will inevitably notice they are happening—and wonder how or if you should intercede. As with the advice given to victims of a microaggression, you have the option to respond in the moment or later on, or let it go.

There is no one right approach to dealing with microaggressions, but here are a few considerations for when you witness one:

1. What's the right moment to say something?

Consider the environment and be thoughtful about how to create a safe space for the conversation. Think about whether the conversation is best had in the moment (possibly in front of other people) or one-on-one.

In some situations, an in-the-moment approach may be sufficient. For example, if someone accidentally misgenders a colleague in a meeting, a leader could say, "Let's make sure we are using everyone's correct pronouns," and keep the meeting going. Doing this can make it less taboo to point out microaggressions and help to create a culture of positive in-the-moment correction when they happen.

But no one likes to be put on the spot, and conversations are much more likely to turn tense if your colleague feels like you are calling them out. So if you need to confront someone, try to "call them in" by creating a safe environment where you can engage the person in honest, authentic dialogue—without a client or other colleagues present—to say, "Hey, I know you didn't mean it this way, but let's not use language like . . . "

2. What's your relationship to the person who made the comment?

Do you have a personal relationship with the person who committed the microaggression? If so, you might be able to simply say, "Hey, you made a comment earlier that did not sit well with me."

However, if you do not have a personal relationship with the colleague, you may want to consider what you know about their personality (do they tend to be combative?) and history with uncomfortable conversations (are they generally approachable?). You may also need to bring in other colleagues they are closer with.

3. What's your personal awareness of the microaggression's subject?

Be honest about your level of familiarity with the subject at hand. For example, maybe you recognize that a comment is a racial microaggression, but you do not know the history or full implications of it. In that case, it's OK to talk to the person, but recognize you are not an authority on the topic, and consider learning more first or talking to someone who has more familiarity with the topic.

Once you realize a microaggression has been committed and you decide to act, it's important to remind your friends or colleagues of the difference between *intent* and *impact*. While the speaker may not have intended the comment to be offensive, we must acknowledge the impact of our statements. Intent does not supersede or excuse actual impact. For example, you could say to the person, "I know you may have intended your statement to come off as _____, but the way I received it was _____." Sometimes simply highlighting the gap between intent and impact can be enlightening for the other person.

If you realize you have committed a microaggression

If someone tells you that you have said something offensive, this is an obvious moment to pause and consider the best way to handle the situation. Using your emotional intelligence, here are some steps to take.

Take a moment to pause

Being called out can put us on the defensive, so breathe deeply and remember that everyone makes mistakes. In most cases committing a microaggression does not mean you are bad person; it signals that you have a chance to treat a colleague with greater respect and to grow on your diversity, equity, and inclusion journey.

Taking a moment to pause, breathe, and reflect can help you avoid reacting with emotion and potentially saying something rash that could make the situation worse.

Ask for clarification

If you are unsure what you did to offend your colleague, invite dialogue by asking for clarification. Say, "Could you say more about what you mean by that?"

Listen for understanding

Listen to your colleague's perspective, even when you disagree. Far too often in uncomfortable conversations, we listen for the opportunity to speak and insert our own opinions instead of truly listening for understanding. To make sure you have understood your colleague's point of view, you could restate or paraphrase what you heard: "I think I heard you saying _____ [paraphrase their comments]. Is that correct?"

Acknowledge and apologize

Once you process that harm has been done, you must acknowledge the offense and sincerely apologize for your statement. This is a moment to be honest, whether you lacked the knowledge of a certain word's history or made a comment that was insensitive. You could say something like, "I can now better understand how I was wrong in this situation. I will work to become more aware of _____ [the topic that you need to increase your cultural awareness of]."

Create space for follow-up

The majority of these tough conversations take more than one conversation to work through. Allow yourself and your colleagues the opportunity to follow up in the future to continue the conversation, especially when cooler heads can prevail. You may say something like, "I would be happy to talk about this more in the future if you have any follow-up thoughts. I appreciate you taking the time to share your perspective with me."

What leaders should know

While microaggressions often happen at the individual level, companies that say they are committed to inclusion should have zero tolerance for exclusionary or discriminatory language toward any employee. Leaders should set the standard by providing training on topics such as microaggressions. Yet, because of the insidious nature of microaggressions, leaders and HR professionals have the responsibility to correct individuals when they become aware that these offenses have happened.

Many microaggressions can become part of an organization's culture if not corrected. For example, I have worked with some organizations where confusing people of the same race happened often and was casually overlooked as an honest mistake. While we all do make mistakes, when these same types of incidents happen consistently to the same groups of people, leaders need to correct the behavior. One client came to me with the issue that two Asian women on the same team were often called each other's name, giving them a feeling of interchangeability. I helped the client share with the firm some tools on how to politely correct someone in the moment, as well as provided some general reminders to the firm about why it's offensive to confuse two people of the same race. One thing that firm did was to push employees to learn each other's names and make sure to have individual interactions with new colleagues to get to know them. They even had a name challenge, with a prize, when they returned to the office after working remotely during the pandemic. In this way, the firm acted to not only call out inappropriate behavior but also shift the culture by making it clear that knowing colleagues' names was an important expectation for all team members.

Ultimately, getting better at noticing and responding to microaggressions—and at being more aware of our everyday speech—is a journey, one with a real effect on our mental health and well-being at work. Microaggressions affect everyone, so creating more inclusive and culturally competent workplace cultures means each of us must explore our own biases in order to become aware of them. The goal is not to be fearful of communicating with each other, but instead to embrace the opportunity to be intentional about it. Creating inclusive cultures where people can thrive does not happen overnight. It takes a continuous process of learning, evolving, and growing.

ELLA F. WASHINGTON is an organizational psychologist; the founder and CEO of Ellavate Solutions, a DEI strategy firm; a professor of practice at Georgetown University's McDonough School of Business; and a cohost of Gallup's Center of Black Voices *Cultural Competence* podcast. She is the author of *The Necessary Journey: Making Real Progress on Equity and Inclusion* (Harvard Business Review Press, 2022).

Note

1. "Understanding Racial Microaggression and Its Effect on Mental Health," Pfizer.com, August 26, 2020, https://www.pfizer.com/news/articles/understanding_racial_microaggression_and_its_effect_on_mental_health.

Adapted from "Recognizing and Responding to Microaggressions at Work" on hbr.org, May 10, 2022 (product #H07195).

6

Tap into Empathy

By Irina Cozma

T reat others as you would like to be treated."

How often did you hear this phrase while growing up? After stealing another kid's toy or hurting someone's feelings, your parents were likely quick to remind you of the "Golden Rule." For many of us, this was our first introduction to the concept of empathy. And there's a good chance you're still (consciously or unconsciously) using this phrase as a guidepost for how you show up.

But in our modern workplace, with all our different preferences, cultural backgrounds, professional disciplines, ages, genders, sexual orientations, and so on, treating others as *you* would like to be treated isn't always the best option. Although it can be help-ful to put yourself in someone else's shoes, doing so can actually lead to making assumptions based on your own perspective—not theirs.

It's time to adopt the "New Golden Rule": Treat others as *they* would like to be treated. It's a small change, but one that can make a huge difference. All it takes to put this new mindset into practice is understanding, curiosity, and compromise.

Challenge your assumptions

I'm an introvert, I enjoy working from my home of-fice, and I find Zoom easier than face-to-face meet-ings. This setting suits me well and makes me feel comfortable. All other introverts must feel the same way, right?

Of course not! The fact that I and other intro-verts share this one personality trait does not mean we all want or like the same things. This is important to keep in mind when implementing the New Golden Rule.

Remember: We are all a unique mix of genetics, experiences, and desires. Even if you share the same personality traits, hobbies, interests, background, or generation as someone, it doesn't mean they think exactly the same way as you. This is even more true when considering the preferences of those you differ from.

When you find yourself making assumptions about another person, ask: Where are these beliefs coming from? What information am I missing? Why do I think my assumptions are true? Are there any alternative explanations or possibilities? Are my assumptions based on my own experiences and understanding of the world, and if so, am I being biased?

Generalizing other people and their characters can be very dangerous—and more often than not, our generalizations are inaccurate.

Ask questions and listen

Imagine this scenario: You're hosting a Zoom meeting and one of your colleagues joins with their camera off. What assumptions run through your mind? Is something wrong? Maybe they don't feel well today. Are they going to multitask during your conversation?

You personally like having your camera on—doing so helps you pay closer attention, holds you accountable, and makes you feel more connected with your colleagues. Why wouldn't they want the same?

You can see just how quickly your assumptions can take over. That's why the best way to really find out how someone else would like to be treated is to simply ask. For example, in this case, you could ask the members of your team if they prefer cameras on or off during meetings and use that information to create a policy that keeps everyone comfortable and on the same page.

Some other sample questions that might be helpful to ask those around you include:

- "How do you prefer to communicate—email or Slack?"

- "Is now still a good time for us to connect?"

- "I'm not sure what you meant when you said [statement]. Can you tell me a little more about it?"

- "In what format do you need the information about this project?"

Not everyone will take the initiative to ask these questions, so when in doubt, don't be afraid to let others know directly about your own preferences. Assumptions can be misleading. Disclosing our preferences and asking more questions can help eliminate misunderstandings.

Replace "or" with "and"

Moving beyond assumptions and taking into consideration what others prefer isn't about putting aside your own needs. When our preferences differ from others, it's essential to look for a solution that works for everyone involved.

Take the virtual meeting scenario. Your colleague prefers to have their camera off. You prefer to have yours on. That arrangement works well for both of you—it doesn't have to be their way versus your way. The more you can accommodate the preferences of the most people involved, the better. So whenever you find yourself in a seemingly "or" situation, take a step back and look for an "and."

Of course, you will at some point find yourself in a situation where compromise isn't possible. If that's the case, it's best to look for any common denominator. You might not be able to agree on everything but try agreeing on just one thing. Look for that small win-win.

We all need to be more cognizant when making generalizations and assumptions. When we rely too heavily on our own perspectives, we miss out on the diverse and important viewpoints around us. Adopting the New Golden Rule will help us all feel more seen and heard.

IRINA COZMA is a career and executive coach who supports professionals to have better career adventures. She has coached hundreds of *Fortune* 500 executives from global organizations like Salesforce, Hitachi, and Abbott. Irina also coaches startups and the Physicians MBA at the University of Tennessee. Download her free career guide at irinacozma .com/career-guide to help you prepare for your next career adventure.

Adapted from "It's Time to Stop Following 'The Golden Rule,'" on Ascend, on hbr.org, August 2, 2022.

7

Inclusion Starts with Belonging

By DDS Dobson-Smith

Humans are social creatures. We have a deep-seated need to be liked, respected, and accepted by our peers. Sometimes that need is so strong, it drives us to alter our behaviors in exchange for approval. At work, school, and other social institutions, this happens every day. People whose identities don't conform with the dominant group are often pressured to present disingenuously to "fit in." Under these circumstances, a sense of belonging is hard to come by.

As an example, let's say that you work at an organization that hires and creates products representative of predominantly white, straight, cisgender, male, able-bodied, middle-class, and thin men. Let's say that you have few of these qualities. Do you feel comfortable walking into the room? Probably not. In fact, you probably feel that you should hide certain parts of yourself to appear less "different." A mother walks into this office and doesn't talk about her children because she thinks it will limit her growth opportunities. A queer person walks into this office and hesitates to mention their same-sex relationship to avoid judgment. A Black man walks into this office and hides how scared they are by another racially driven murder in the news because who will be able to relate to and understand that feeling?

If you look, sound, love, or think differently than the majority in the spaces you occupy, then you already know this. You also know that it comes at a cost—emotionally, physically, and mentally.

While the issue here is systemic and ultimately needs to be solved at the leadership level, you don't have to sit by until change knocks. The experience of belonging is unique in that it doesn't only come down to your organization, your manager, or your team-mates. You have a role to play, too, and that role starts with self-acceptance.

Discover your power

Every one of us has the power to accept and honor who we are at our core. This looks like owning our qualities, values, and choices regardless of how we think others will perceive us, and showing up for and believing in ourselves first.

Self-acceptance happens through the process of self-discovery and self-awareness. It's a state we experience when we welcome, include, and take pride in all that we are and all that we're not yet. When we welcome every part of ourselves, the pressure to perform or suppress our true characters lifts. We create more space to exist comfortably within and can give more—to our work, to our customers, and to our relationships—in that space.

It's only when we *like* ourselves, and care for ourselves like we would a loved one, that we begin to feel that we deserve to be visible and feel we belong.

What gets in the way of self-acceptance?

While society is one factor that gets in the way, we do, too. Self-acceptance may be essential to our well-being, our happiness, and our work, but it's not something we can conquer overnight. It requires regular practice to overcome the biases many of us have been taught to hold against ourselves since childhood. To understand why this is, we have to go back to the beginning.

Most infants and young children are developing at lightning speed—faster than our adult brain can imagine. As babies, basic connections are made in our brains, synapses are created, and we absorb information indiscriminately and without discernment. The majority of this knowledge arrives through interactions with our immediate caretakers, family, and friends. As we grow older, that circle expands to our schools, religious institutions, workplaces, communities, and the media—pop culture and the practices, beliefs, and objects trending at any given time.

By adolescence, most of us have learned (subconsciously or consciously) what our society promotes and favors. In most cultures, this manifests as a set of inborn characteristics or identity markers. For example, right now, and for centuries in the United States, the dominant group identity markers include white, male, cisgender, heterosexual, and able-bodied.

When you consider that, from the start, we're trained to believe certain characteristics are "in" or "out," good or less good, favorable or unfavorable, the battle with self-acceptance becomes easier to understand. This training is further compounded by the way historically marginalized identities have been portrayed in mainstream media: the Asian person as the underdog, the Black person as the criminal, the trans person as the lovesick loner, the gay person as the drug-fueled partygoer, or the disabled person as the butt of the joke.

For anyone who is not a member of the dominant groups—and sometimes even for those who are— we internalize these messages when we are young and create beliefs about what is and what isn't good, right, and likable. Inevitably, we end up projecting those biases onto ourselves, creating negative self-images, and low expectations of our capabilities. These projections, or internalized prejudices, become calcified as our personal truths. They are weapons we unknowingly use against ourselves, causing us emotional pain, holding us back from achieving our full potential, and suppressing our experience of pride.

This is the source of the oft-talked about, and universally experienced, phenomenon known as impostor syndrome, the cause of many derailed lives and careers. This is also why, as adults, we need to do the work to unlearn our own biases, especially the ones we have against ourselves. That work isn't going to be easy. It's going to be very hard.

While I agree that this is a societal problem at large, know that we have the tools to thrive under the circumstances we find ourselves in. Here is some advice on how to take back power by rewriting your individual narratives and beliefs, and developing the kind of thoughts and habits that will create change for the future.

Start by learning to love yourself

If you have at least one identity marker that comes from a marginalized or underrepresented group, it isn't so much a case of *if* you have internalized sexism, racism, ableism, transphobia, or homophobia, but more a case of *how* it shows up and impacts your inner and outer worlds. The good news is that it's possible to unlearn your biases and relearn to love all the parts of who you are, despite what the dominant discourse would have you believe.

Based on my experience as a licensed therapist and executive coach, here are a few tips to help you get started.

Breathe

The idea that you might be holding yourself back due to internalized prejudice is a challenging concept to get your head around. Sit quietly and breathe deeply and consciously as you let your thoughts surface into awareness.

Focused breathing will keep you grounded instead of getting lost in your thoughts or becoming dysregulated emotionally. Your deep breaths slow your active mind and allow you to look more deeply into what you're feeling. Connecting with your breath and your body is important when confronting internalized prejudice and beginning a process of self-discovery.

Do a life audit

Internalized prejudice is caused by the environment that you're in—the books you read, the TV shows you watch, who you follow in your social feeds, and the people you hang out with. So, do an audit of your environment. Are you surrounding yourself with people and things that validate your identity? Does your environment make you feel inferior or powerful?

Make it a priority to fill your life (at work and at home) with influences that are supportive of you. At work, get in touch with your organization's employee resource groups (ERGs) to connect with people who represent your intersectional identity. If your employer doesn't provide ERGs, then undertake a search in your local area for peer support groups, clubs, or associations that are devoted to people like you.

At home, look at your friend groups, the content you're consuming, and the experiences you're seeking on social media. Make sure these areas of your life are abundant, energizing, and affirming—not draining.

Educate yourself about yourself

When you internalize myths and misinformation about your identity, you may (often unconsciously) feel that you aren't as worthy as people in the dominant group.[1] You may act in ways that reinforce this belief and hold you back from being yourself in uncomfortable spaces, like work. Hence, awareness is essential.

To unlearn the biased lessons imposed during your upbringing, you need to reteach yourself the truth about our (and your) history. Learning more about the societal structures that uphold oppression and exclusion will help you reframe your internalized prejudice through uncovering their origins. Further, learning the history of your communities, and how the people who came before you fought the odds, is the first step to gaining self-awareness, which leads to empowerment and acceptance.

For example, everything we have learned has been subject to the bias and perspectives of the lesson-giver, whether that be a family member, a teacher at middle school, a book we borrowed from the library, or a YouTube video we watched. In the process of ed-ucating yourself about yourself, you must be willing to unlearn, and you must be willing to be uncomfort-able; allowing truths to become untruths in the pro-cess of expanding your map of the world isn't always easy. My advice here is simple: Don't believe every-thing you think. Learn to question your own opinions by challenging where and who they come from, and asking yourself what evidence you have to prove or disprove them.

Some people choose to do this work with a ther-apist who can provide a loving, supportive, and objective space. Other people choose self-reflective journaling as a way to track their thoughts and emotions over time, and many people choose to do both. To open the door to unlearning (and relearning), I recommend three great podcasts from the Scene on Radio series—*Seeing White*, *Men*, and *The Land That Has Never Been Yet*—as informative, factual, and powerful sources of insight and learning. Another great podcast from NPR, *Hidden Brain: "Man Up,"* is also worth checking out.

Be kind to yourself

Unpacking and exploring your internalized prejudice may surface unpleasant memories or associations; it can be hard and lead to feelings of shame, guilt, and embarrassment. To that end, please do this work with self-compassion and empathy. Know that your difficult feelings are valid and are a part of your healing and self-acceptance process. Don't run away from them. Instead, get curious about how and why they've developed. This is the only way to grow and be kinder to yourself in the future.

————————

Belonging is an archetypal experience that all humans seek, whoever they are. It transcends geographies, generations, and genotypes. When we recognize that we're not alone in our desire to belong, then we can live with greater empathy—empathy not only for others, but also for ourselves. And it is with that spirit of empathy for ourselves that we can gently and kindly dismantle any internalized prejudice and open up into greater levels of self-acceptance.

DDS DOBSON-SMITH is a licensed therapist, author, executive coach, expert on leadership development, and Reiki master—all in service of helping others grow and become who they are. They are the founder of SoulTrained, an executive coaching and leadership growth consultancy, and the author of two books: *You Can Be Yourself Here: Your Pocket Guide to*

Creating Inclusive Workplaces by Using the Psychology of Belonging and *Leadership Is a Behavior Not a Title: Your Pocket Guide to Being a Leader Worth Following.* Learn more at www.soultrained.com.

Note

1. "Section 3. Healing from the Effects of Internalized Oppression, Chapter 27. Working Together for Racial Justice and Inclusion," Cultural Competence and Spirituality in Community Building, Community Toolbox, Center for Community Health and Development at the University of Kansas, https://ctb.ku.edu/en/table-of-contents/culture/cultural-competence/healing-from-interalized-oppression/main.

Adapted from "A Sense of Belonging Starts with Self-Acceptance," on Ascend, on hbr.org, August 8, 2022.

8

Stop Using These Words and Phrases

By Rakshitha Arni Ravishankar

Try this thought experiment: You're sitting at your desk when your friend texts you an article about a topic you're passionate about. You read it and ask her what she thinks. To your surprise, her opinion is the complete opposite of yours. This obviously upsets you. Later that evening, as you explain what happened to your partner, how do you describe your friend's point of view?

If you said it was "stupid," "insane," "crazy," "lame," or "dumb," you have (unknowingly or not) participated in spreading ableist language.

You may be surprised to learn that your response was a form of discrimination. People use ableist words and phrases every day without realizing the harm they do.

Ableism is defined as discrimination or social prejudice against people with disabilities based on the belief that typical abilities are superior. It can manifest as an attitude, stereotype, or an outright offensive comment or behavior. When it comes to language, ableism often shows up as metaphors ("My boyfriend is *emotionally crippled*"), jokes ("That comedian was *hysterical*"), and euphemisms ("He is *differently abled*") in conversation.

As a journalist with a background in media studies, I spend a lot of time thinking about language and the words we choose to express ourselves. Our words, and the reasons why we choose them, reflect the times we live in. Just as some historically racist, sexist, and derogatory terms have been retired, so have a handful of ableist slurs that were used to dehumanize, stigmatize, and institutionalize people in the past. At the same time, too many people continue to casually spew ableist language to ridicule, criticize, or dismiss others.

My intent is not to shame anyone; it is to help more people understand how to identify and stop using words and phrases that reinforce ableism. I reached out to several disability rights advocates for their insights.

Here's what I learned.

Ableism is bigger than language

Language is a tool we use to make sense of our feelings and environment. When we verbally describe the things, experiences, and people around us, we are also assigning value to them and that value impacts how we interact with each other.

Ableist language largely influences us in three ways.

1. It reveals our unconscious biases

Lydia X. Z. Brown, a disability justice advocate, told me that our attitudes toward disability show up in the language we use. "If we believe people with mental illness should not be in our workplace, life, family, or neighborhood, then, it's easier to rationalize using ableist words," Brown said. "You might think: 'Only crazy people do that. I don't do that, so it's okay for me to say.' But when people say these things, they send a signal to people with psychosocial disabilities that we are not welcome."

Of course, Brown noted, that language is just one way ableism shows up. "By removing ableism from your vocabulary, you don't remove ableism from your surroundings."

Ableism can be blatant, especially in work or school environments. It could be the lack of accessible infrastructures, or something more insidious, like performance evaluations based on what are traditionally considered "productive" or "appropriate" behaviors.

Shain Neumeier, a lawyer and activist, added, "Unfortunately, people may not realize that doodling during a meeting [or class] may be your way of paying attention, especially if you're someone with an invisible disability. They might just think it's an abnormal behavior for that space."

2. It makes us internalize harmful biases about disability

When you treat a disability as a joke, metaphor, or euphemism, you are causing harm in a couple of ways. First, you are spreading the idea that it's acceptable to dehumanize and stigmatize someone with a disability. Depending on your circle or friend group, you could even be enabling others to do the same.

Second, a disabled person may end up internalizing those tropes themselves. "The first time someone makes fun of you or people like you (even if it's not directed at you), it's a little drop in the bucket. It's like a poke," Neumeier said. "But, when you are put down

100 times, over and over again, you start feeling disrespected, and it becomes hard to be around the perpetrators. Specifically in the work environment, if there is an imbalanced power dynamic, and the perpetrator is your boss, it can be very difficult."

Neumeier also pointed out that writing off a slur or universally unacceptable expression—like the r-word or the m-word—may be easier for a disabled person than constantly confronting microaggressions. If the person facing discrimination doesn't have a support system, they may start to believe something is wrong with them, and that's dangerous.

3. It stigmatizes already marginalized people

Allilsa Fernandez, a mental health and disability activist, told me that using words that are ableist can distract attention from the point you're trying to make and normalize the idea that disabilities equate to insults. Fernandez explained, "When you say

Trump is such a 'psycho' or 'weirdo' for his stance on immigration, you end up focusing on those specific words, without addressing the real issue: what it is that you don't like about the immigration policy."

If you want to critique a politician's viewpoint or an administration's policy (or anything for that matter), Fernandez advises that you talk about the reasons you agree or disagree with it. "When you attack a person's physical and mental abilities in place of actually expressing an opinion or idea, you further stigmatize people with disabilities," said Fernandez.

A conscious effort to improve your vocabulary

Using ableist language doesn't make you a bad person. It makes you a person. But, if you have the privilege to change your vocabulary for the better, then why not try?

I asked my interviewees for a few beginner tips. This was their advice.

1. Acknowledge the disability around you

More than 1 billion people worldwide, around 15% of the population, have some type of disability.[1] People with disabilities make up a quarter of the U.S. population.[2]

Professor Beth Haller teaches disability and media studies at Towson University. She told me the more conscious we become of the disability around us, the less we are likely to stigmatize it as *something to be fixed* and look at it as *something that is.*

"Usually, people exist on two ends: People either feel bad for you if you are disabled or self-aggrandize by feeling 'lucky' for the life they live (without the disability)," she explained. "Both of those things are unhelpful."

Haller said that, as a world, we need to get out of the mindset that a disabled person has "less than the rest of us." That's where the discrimination begins.

Pro tip: Don't try to fix disability; instead fix the oppression.

2. Learn, learn, learn

"Education, that's where you start," Fernandez says. "It's not that people don't stop and think about the impact their words have on others, it's just that language is very deeply ingrained. It reflects our families, friends, cultures, and identity." According to Fernandez, becoming aware of our own biases—many of which we've picked up from the people we've met, the experiences we've had, and the media we've consumed throughout our lives—is the first step to educating ourselves.

Another way to become more aware of our own biases is to listen more than we talk. Neumeier told me to think of listening as a means of building stronger relationships—at work or beyond. "Look at every interaction you have as a way to bond with others, rather than just a clash of ideas. Otherwise, we are all going to feel isolated."

Finally, Brown added that it's important for everyone to use the resources put out by disabled people. "Look for articles, books, videos, podcasts, and other work by disabled writers and activists. Use these tools to learn about the way discrimination or ableism works." Doing so will help you recognize when it's happening in real life—whether it's coming from you, or someone else.

Pro tip: Educate yourself, and don't rely on others to teach you.

3. Don't make assumptions about someone's identity

Linguistic rules are evolving. In the late 1980s and early '90s, during the AIDS epidemic, organizations began to move away from words like "handicapped" and embrace what is referred to as people-first language, according to Haller. Instead of defining people by their disability, the movement sought to focus on the fact that people with disabilities are, first and foremost, just people. An example of this would be saying "a person with a disability" instead of "a disabled person."

This was the linguistic rule for some time. Then, in the early '90s, other disability communities, like the National Federation of the Blind and the d/Deaf community, mobilized for an identity-first rule so disability could be recognized as an identity and not just a medical category. For instance, some individuals may prefer "Deaf" (capitalized) instead of "people who are deaf" or "people with loss of hearing."

The history behind our identities and how we name them is complex. "Today, the best strategy is just to ask people how they want to be addressed," Haller said.

Everyone I interviewed echoed this sentiment: clarifying questions about identity shows respect.

Pro tip: The best rule is: When you're unsure of someone's identity, just ask.

4. When you make a mistake, genuinely apologize

"When someone tells you that something is disrespectful, you don't have to understand why they are hurt. Just that they are," said Brown. "I love cooking for my friends. But, if someone says they didn't like a dish I made for them, then I'm not going to force them to eat it. I don't have to understand or argue or even agree with them. But if I have a choice, why would I make my friend a dish they don't like?"

Brown cautions to be aware of your reaction if someone calls you out. Getting defensive may be a natural response, but the last thing you want to do is make someone else's pain about you, even if you had good intentions. Instead, genuinely check yourself, say you're sorry, and do better in the future.

Pro tip: This isn't about your opinions; it's about how the other person feels.

My big takeaway from these conversations is that the pain and isolation that accompany discrimination and prejudice run much deeper than the ableist words many of us were taught as kids. Those words hurt people, and that hurt is valid.

The upside is that history shows us that language and communications evolve. This means we have a lot of room to create vocabularies that are more empowering and inclusive—ones that address historical injustices and make everybody feel welcome.

Language isn't meant to alienate us; it's meant to help us understand one another.

RAKSHITHA ARNI RAVISHANKAR is an associate editor at HBR Ascend.

Notes

1. "Disability Inclusion," World Bank, April 14, 2022, https://www.worldbank.org/en/topic/disability.
2. "Disability Impacts All of Us," Centers for Disease Control and Prevention, https://www.cdc.gov/ncbddd/disability andhealth/infographic-disability-impacts-all.html.

Adapted from "Why You Need to Stop Using These Words and Phrases" on Ascend, on hbr.org, December 15, 2020.

9

The Power
of Sharing
Our Stories

By Selena Rezvani and Stacey A. Gordon

As inclusion consultants, we see more and more companies doubling down on diversity metrics like business cases, scorecards, and targets. After all, what matters gets measured, right?

These programs track things like workforce demographics, diversity hiring, retention, promotion rates, and utilization of DEI resources. While those measures have their place, we've found that they're insufficient to create inclusion on their own. In fact, an overly mathematical approach actually de-emphasizes the very thing we hope to build in inclusive workplaces: awareness, connection, empathy, and mutual respect.

In our attempts to create more awake and aware environments, we're forgetting that numbers typically don't inspire us to change our behavior—people and stories do. With our corporate clients, it's the exchange of human experiences via stories, focus groups, and listening sessions that tend to inspire lasting change for people on a personal level.

We can make actual progress on inclusion by implementing a story-based approach where employees are encouraged to tell their stories, own them, and consider how they impact their day-to-day experiences at work.

Whose stories get told?

So now you might be thinking: If we're going to tell more stories, it makes sense to start with leaders, right?

Not necessarily.

One study published in the *Academy of Management Journal* revealed that newcomers prefer to hear stories from their peers rather than leaders.[1] If that's true, why do most inclusion programs leave so little space for peers to share their lived experiences?

It's up to leaders to facilitate that sharing. Failure to do so leaves employees, especially women and people of color, feeling unrepresented. One of our clients at a consumer goods company called us because women weren't "raising their hands" for opportunities at the same rate as men. After dozens of one-on-one interviews, we found that women *had* been raising their hands—and were continually being passed over and dismissed. We then facilitated a session with leaders and employees, presenting themes from their interviews. A principal at the company called it the most raw, honest dialogue they'd experienced in years, thanks to the unfiltered stories and voices of employees.

When people hear stories that feel representative, it creates a vehicle for nuanced conversations, which are what truly drive change. Stories invite perspective-taking: the concept of standing in someone else's shoes and imagining what it's like to be them. It's a drastically underutilized inclusion tool. One study found that taking the perspective of others "may have a lasting positive effect on diversity-related outcomes by increasing individuals' internal motivation to respond without prejudice."[2]

One CEO we worked with in the entertainment industry didn't really understand what ERGs are or why the company needed them. Still, he signed off on starting them and even allocated some budget for them. He was skeptical and didn't see the point *until* he attended one of the events held by the LGBTQ ERG and heard, through stories, how bias affected those employees. Later, he heard how much happier they were at work once they began feeling as though they belonged, and they began working on ways to improve the company—not just for LGBTQ employees, but for everyone.

Look in the mirror

Because traditional DEI programs can make things too abstract and overlook the fact that DEI is about the people, we tell all leaders—even cisgender, white, heterosexual men—to first look in the mirror and examine their own diversity stories. Doing this work helps leaders understand and empathize with the narratives shared by others. Once they uncover their own stories, they may be invited (and expected) to share their own—in addition to, not over and above, the stories of individual contributors.

People crave authenticity, texture, and transparency in leaders. They don't want the diluted, professional version of who you are. There's a false narrative that our unique and personal backgrounds are somehow unprofessional and should never be addressed at work. But, regardless of whether we ignore them or bring them to the fore, they shape the way we interact with others in every situation—nobody is ever fully objective. Bringing our own stories to the table helps us create contrast with others and better see the nuance in ours and their perspectives.

If you feel stuck or unsure of how to dig into your own diversity story, here are few prompts to get you started:

- When did your privilege afford you different treatment than someone else?

- When did someone advocate for you? (Did someone with privilege help you?)

- Did you ever need to search to find your own sense of belonging?

- When did you discover a bias or privilege you had and how did you overcome it?

- Have you ever felt pressure to conform or fit in?

- Did you ever witness an unconscious bias play out in the workplace?

Here's what we learned from this exercise ourselves:

> *Selena:* "As a biracial person, I dismissed and minimized my personal diversity stories for so long. I'm half-Pakistani and brown-presenting—and also half-Caucasian and at times white-passing. Being mixed can make you feel like you don't belong anywhere. Once I finally told my story about the contrasts that I experience being multiethnic, I felt a sense of freedom that allowed me to connect with others—even clients—more deeply and authentically."

> *Stacey:* "As a Black person in a white world, growing up as one of very few Black children

in my school, I never felt that I fit in. I thought that would change when I moved to Brooklyn, New York, but surprisingly, it didn't. Because once I arrived, I realized everyone saw me as 'the British girl.' It took years to embrace my nontraditional culture, but owning my background helped me gain that sense of belonging, and now I use that journey to help our clients do the same."

More than 500 professionals responded to our organization's DEI Blueprint survey, and only 4% of respondents were able to answer in the affirmative that "[o]ur leadership is aligned on the commitment to diversity and inclusion in the organization."[3] How can leaders show up and tell their stories if there's no alignment on the importance of DEI? That's a gaping disconnect, and a *big* problem. It means the stories we hear from them are often watered down and unrelatable. They don't serve a purpose, they're just lip service, and they don't help people see the leader's humanity.

So, what's a leader to do?

Share! Share your story as authentically as possible. Share how it made you feel. Share the mistakes you've made. Be honest.

Create space for storytelling

The best way to create a cascading inclusion effect in an organization is to offer safe spaces where stories can be heard without judgment. This works best when psychological safety is being actively cultivated. There is a natural give-and-take to storytelling—a vulnerability that comes with sharing—and an instinct to reciprocate. That means that in the most psychologically safe workplaces, people aren't *required* to share, but they're *safe* to share. The vulnerability employees are placing in leaders' hands has to be cared for by the organization. To encourage team members to talk regularly about their diversity stories, consider the following actions:

- Do a round-robin question in a meeting.

- Hold listening sessions.

- Host discussion-heavy book clubs.

- Schedule storytelling town halls.

- Include stories in blogs, videos, celebrations, promotions, and onboarding.

- Be transparent about surveys and focus groups that show negative perceptions and harmful treatment.

- Have social forums and meetups.

- Develop dynamic social media campaigns that share stories.

Many people may be walking around with powerful experiences but don't see them as "good stories." Reassure them that their stories don't need to be perfect, they just need to be *real*.

As you open up forums for your team, encourage people to tell their stories in their own words by:

- *Bringing a beginner's mindset.* Let go of what you *think* you know so you can actively listen to what is being said.

- *Receiving diversity stories with empathy and warmth.* Affirm the stories you hear, even if you don't relate or completely understand how a person feels. If someone is emotional or uncomfortable, affirm that you're there to support them.

- *Not asking storytellers to " oververify."* After someone is done sharing, even if you have questions, don't challenge or ask people to give evidence for their stories. If you do have questions, ask them directly if you can pose a follow-up question about their experience when they're done.

- *Thanking people for sharing.* It's important to let people know that you hear them and appreciate them sharing.

- *Checking in about continually improving safe spaces.* As more storytelling forums take place, check in with people. Ask if they feel you've created a space where people can tell their stories and be heard.

———

It's time for the conversation around inclusion and diversity to take a human-centric approach. It's not just about the numbers—it's about the *people*. Storytelling, one of the most universal human experiences, gives us a rare chance to look through new lenses. And perspective-taking is a life skill, not just a workplace one. Companies that prioritize inclusion will emerge from crisis stronger, and stories are one major vehicle to help them get there.

SELENA REZVANI consults with employers on how to make work truly "work" for women—through cultural diagnostics, focus groups, and by implementing cutting-edge inclusion programs. Selena is the author of two leadership books, *Pushback* and *The Next Generation of Women Leaders*, and the forthcoming *Quick Confidence*. In 2019, Selena's TEDx talk, "Interrupting Gender Bias Through Meeting Culture," was recognized with the Croly Journalism award. To learn more, visit www.selenarezvani.com. STACEY A. GORDON is a workplace culture consultant, keynote speaker, author, facilitator of learning, and executive adviser on diversity strategies. As the founder of Rework Work, she coaches leaders to lead workplaces where all stakeholders #WorkTogether to create belonging. Stacey's unconscious bias course is number one on the LinkedIn Learning platform and has been translated into several languages. She is also the author of *UNBIAS: Addressing Unconscious Bias at Work*. To learn more, visit learn.reworkwork.com.

Notes

1. Sean R. Martin, "Stories About Values and Valuable Stories: A Field Experiment of the Power of Narratives to Shape Newcomers' Actions," *Academy of Management Journal* 59, no. 5 (2015), https://journals.aom.org/doi/10.5465/amj.2014.0061.
2. Alex Lindsey et al., "The Impact of Method, Motivation, and Empathy on Diversity Training Effectiveness," *Journal of Business and Psychology* 30 (2015): 605–617.
3. "Diversity Equity & Inclusion Workplace Assessment," https://www.reworkwork.com/about-us/workplace-assessment/.

Adapted from "How Sharing Our Stories Builds Inclusion" on hbr.org, November 1, 2021 (product #H06NYO).

Index

ableism/ableist language,
117–130
improving vocabulary,
123–129
internalizing harmful biases,
121–122
and language use, 119
lessons learned from,
129–130
revealing unconscious biases,
120–121
stigmatizing marginalized
people, 122–123
*Academy of Management
Journal*, 135
accountability, for psychological
safety, 44–45
allyship, 24–25, 26, 43
alternative views, 9
apologizing, 83, 128–129
awareness of bias, 5, 86, 125–
126. *See also* self-awareness

beginner's mindset, 143
being kind, to yourself,
112–113
belonging, 38, 101–113
difficulties in experiencing,
101–103
learning to love yourself,
107–113
self-acceptance, 103–107
social, 17–18
at work. *See* workplace
belonging
BetterUp studies, 18, 19
bias(es), 101–103
awareness of, 5, 86, 125–126
internalization of, about
disability, 121–122
self-acceptance to overcome,
104
unconscious, 120–121
unlearning, 107, 110–112
"blacklist," 71

blind spots, of psychological
    safety, 39–40
Bourke, Juliet, 3–12, 51–62
breathing, 81–82, 108–109
Brown, Lydia X. Z., 120, 126,
    128–129

candor, 32, 34, 35
Carr, Evan W., 17–26
Chiaburu, Dan, 61–62
citizenship discrimination,
    73–74
class discrimination, 74
collaboration, 4, 6, 40
Cozma, Irina, 91–97
cultural differences, 8
cultural dimensions for
        resilience
    inclusion, 32, 38–39, 45
    innovation, 32, 36–37, 45
    integrity, 32, 34–36, 45
cultural intelligence, 6
culture, of workplace. *See*
        organizational culture
curiosity about others, 5–6

D&I trainings. *See* diversity and
    inclusion trainings

DEI initiatives. *See* diversity, eq-
    uity, and inclusion initiatives
disability, 120, 127
    ableism and. *See* ableism/
        ableist language
    acknowledging, 124–125
    internalization of biases about,
        121–122
discrimination/discriminatory
        language, 71–72, 84
    ableism as, 117–118, 122, 125,
        126
    citizenship, 73–74
    class, 74
    gender, 75
    mental health, 74–75
    of parental status, 76
    racial/ethnic, 73
    sexual, 75–76
diversity
    among employees, 38–39
    as business strategy, 44
    conversation around,
        144–145
    experiential, 39
    metrics, 133
    organizational, 33
    policies, 51, 61
    recruiting and hiring for, 25
    stories, 137, 138–139, 142, 143

diversity and inclusion trainings (D&I trainings), 10, 17, 44
diversity, equity, and inclusion initiatives (DEI initiatives), 43–44, 82, 137–141
Dobson-Smith, DDS, 101–113

embodied connection, 55–56, 61
emotional care of others, 54–55, 61
empathy, 91–97, 112, 113
employee resource groups (ERGs), 109, 136
employees
  diversity among, 38–39
  excluded, 21–22
  fear of retaliation, 35
  psychological safety of, 58
employer promoter score, 20
empowerment, 23–24
engagement, 17, 38
environment, sustainability, and governance commitments (ESG), 33, 44
ERGs. See employee resource groups
ESG. See environment, sustainability, and governance commitments

ethical business behavior, 33
ethical decision making, clarity in expectations for, 42–43
exclusion, 17–26, 100. See also workplace exclusion
  acts of, by leaders, 10
  allies to prevent, 24–25
  costs of, 20–22
exclusionary language, 84
  interpersonal, 59–61
  interventions for, 23
  reversing effects of, 22–24
external reporting, 36

favoritism, 9
Fernandez, Allilsa, 122–123, 125
focused breathing, 108–109

gaining perspective, 23, 25–26
gender discrimination, 75
"Golden Rule," 91. See also "New Golden Rule"
Gordon, Stacey A., 133–145
groupthink, 38
Gube, Maren, 31–45

Haller, Beth, 124–125, 127
Harrison, David, 61–62
Hennelly, Debra Sabatini, 31–45
humility, 5

impostor syndrome, 106–107
included workers, 21–22
inclusive leadership, 3–12
  definition, 3
  good leadership vs., 6
  getting started in, 10–12
  insights on, 6–8
  traits/behaviors of, 5–6, 8–10
inclusiveness, 3–4, 7
inclusive workplaces, 51, 52,
  69–70, 133
innovation, for psychological
  safety, 32, 36–37
instrumental assistance, 53–54,
  57, 61
integrity, for psychological safety,
  32, 33, 34–36
intent, vs. impact, 80–81
internalized prejudice, 106,
  108–109, 110, 112
interpersonal inclusion, 51–62
  disadvantages of, 59–61
  embodied connection, 55–56,
  61

emotional care of others,
  54–55, 61
instrumental assistance,
  53–54, 57, 61
as reciprocal process, 56–59

journaling, 112

Kellerman, Gabriella Rosen,
  17–26

language. *See* ableism/ableist
  language
leadership, good vs. inclusive, 6.
  See also inclusive leadership
learning
  cultural differences, 8
  importance of, 125–126
learning to love yourself,
  107–108
  being kind to yourself,
  112–113
  doing life audit, 109–110
  internalized prejudice, 106,
  108–109, 110, 112
  unlearning bias from
  upbringing, 110–112

left-out feelings, 25. *See also* exclusion
life audit, 109–110
linguistic rules, 127

"man up," 71, 72
marginalized people, stigmatizing, 122–123
mental health discrimination, 74–75
mentorship, 23–24, 25
microaggressions, 67–86
  acknowledging and apologizing, 83
  approaches to dealing with, 77–81
  asking for clarification, 82
  against Black people, 68
  awareness of, 70–72, 77, 80–81, 84
  creating space for follow-up, 83–84
  creating inclusive workplaces to combat, 69–70
  intent vs. impact of, 80–81
  hurtful words and phrases, 71–77
  leaders' responsibility to manage, 84–86

listening for understanding, 82–83
  negative impact in career, 68–69
  speaking up about, 78–79
  taking time to pause, 81–82

National Federation of the Blind and the d/Deaf community, 127–128
The Necessary Journey (Washington), 70
Neumeier, Shain, 121–122, 126
"New Golden Rule," 92–93

organizational culture
  assessing, 42
  correcting microaggressions in, 70, 78, 85–86
  of curiosity, 37
  inclusive, 10, 61, 86
  of integrity, 34–36
  psychologically safe, 31, 32
organizational diversity, 33
outside-the-box thinking, encouraging, 43
overpowering others, 9

parental status, discrimination
    of, 76
"peanut gallery," 71
peer relationships, 51
  impact on individual's
    experience of inclusion,
    52–53
  interpersonal exclusion and,
    59–61
significance of focusing on,
    61
people-first language, 127
performance metrics, 44–45
personal weaknesses,
    sharing, 8. *See also*
    storytelling
perspective, gaining, 23,
    25–26
perspective-taking, 136, 145
physical connection. *See*
    embodied connection
preferred pronouns, 78
psychological safety, 31–45
  accountability for, 44–45
  blind spots of, 39–40
  cultural dimensions for
    resilience, 32, 34–39
  focus areas for leaders,
    42–45

as foundation of resilience,
    33–34
vulnerability as obstacle of,
    40–41

racial/ethnic discrimination, 73
Ravishankar, Rakshitha Arni,
    117–130
Razzetti, Gustavo, 41
Reece, Andrew, 17–26
Remote, Not Distant (Razzetti),
    41
resilience
  cultural dimensions for, 32,
    34–39, 45
  organizational, 31
  psychological safety as
    foundation of, 33–34
retaliation, fear of, 35–36
Rezvani, Selena, 133–145
Robichaux, Alexi, 17–26

self-acceptance, 103–107, 112
self-awareness, 103, 111
self-compassion, 112
self-sabotage, 21–22
sexual discrimination, 75–76

social belonging, 17–18. *See also* belonging; workplace belonging

storytelling, 133–145
  creating space for, 141–144
  leaders' role in, 137, 140–141
  listening to, 143
  questions to ask yourself, 138–139
  real vs. good, 143
  receiving with empathy, 143

team sabotage, 21–22
Titus, Andrea, 3–12
traits/behaviors, of inclusive leaders, 5–6, 8–10

"upstanders," 36, 43

visible commitment, 5
vocabulary, improving, 123–129
vulnerability, 40–41, 141–142

Washington, Ella F., 67–86
"whitelist," 71
workers. *See* employees
workplace belonging, 17–26
  creating, 25–26
  research, 18–20
  value for business, 20
workplace culture. *See* organizational culture
workplace exclusion, 17–18. *See also* exclusion
  allies as protection from, 24–25
  reversing effects of, 22–24
  sabotage and, 21–22

How to be human at work.

HBR's Emotional Intelligence Series features smart, essential reading on the human side of professional life from the pages of *Harvard Business Review*. Each book in the series offers uplifting stories, practical advice, and research from leading experts on how to tend to our emotional well-being at work.

Harvard Business Review Emotional Intelligence Series

Available in paperback or ebook format. The specially priced six-volume set includes:

- Mindfulness
- Resilience
- Influence and Persuasion

- Authentic Leadership
- Happiness
- Empathy